GARDENING FOR BEGINNERS

Growing Vegetables and Herbs in Small Spaces

(Perennial Vegetables - Plant Once and Harvest Year After Year)

Erma Davis

Published by Harry Barnes

Erma Davis

All Rights Reserved

Gardening for Beginners: Growing Vegetables and Herbs in Small Spaces (Perennial Vegetables - Plant Once and Harvest Year After Year)

ISBN 978-1-77485-141-8

All rights reserved. No part of this guide may be reproduced in any form without permission in writing from the publisher except in the case of brief quotations embodied in critical articles or reviews.

Legal & Disclaimer

The information contained in this book is not designed to replace or take the place of any form of medicine or professional medical advice. The information in this book has been provided for educational and entertainment purposes only.

The information contained in this book has been compiled from sources deemed reliable, and it is accurate to the best of the Author's knowledge; however, the Author cannot guarantee its accuracy and validity and cannot be held liable for any errors or omissions. Changes are periodically made to this book. You must consult your doctor or get professional medical advice before using any of the suggested remedies, techniques, or information in this book.

Upon using the information contained in this book, you agree to hold harmless the Author from and against any damages, costs, and expenses, including any legal fees potentially resulting from the application of any of the information provided by this guide. This disclaimer applies to any damages or injury caused by the use and application, whether directly or indirectly, of any advice or information presented, whether for breach of contract, tort, negligence, personal injury, criminal intent, or under any other cause of action.

You agree to accept all risks of using the information presented inside this book. You need to consult a professional medical practitioner in order to ensure you are both able and healthy enough to participate in this program.

Table of Contents

INTRODUCTION 1

CHAPTER 1: INTRODUCTION TO CONTAINER GARDENING!
.... 13

CHAPTER 2: PREPARING FOR YOUR SQUARE FOOT GARDEN 17

CHAPTER 3: CHOOSING THE RIGHT MEDIUM 31

CHAPTER 4: LAND & THE LANDSCAPE 38

CHAPTER 5: FRUITS 54

CHAPTER 7: PERENNIAL VEGETABLES 62

CHAPTER 8: GARDENING CAN BE EASY 69

CHAPTER 9: PERENNIAL FRUIT BEARING TREES AND BUSHES 73

CHAPTER 10: UNDERSTANDING PLANTS 86

CHAPTER 11: ALL METHODS OF GARDENING SHARE THESE SAME BENEFITS 92

CHAPTER 12: THE BEAUTY OF PERENNIAL VEGETABLES. 101

CHAPTER 13: PREPARING THE TERRACE 121

CHAPTER 14: WHAT IS VERTICIAL GARDENING? 126

CHAPTER 15: LANDSCAPING – AN OVERVIEW 129

CHAPTER 16: UNDERSTANDING HOMESTEADING 140

CHAPTER 17: HELPFUL TIPS IN GARDENING................... 157

CHAPTER 18: HARVESTING AND MAINTENANCE 167

CHAPTER 19: APPRENTICESHIPS 176

CONCLUSION 179

Introduction

Hydroponics is a technique that grows plants in a water-based solution that is rich in nutrients. Hydroponics does not use soil but uses an inert medium to support the root system. Hydroponics science shows that for plant growth, soil is not required, but the elements, minerals, and nutrients contained in soil are required.

The Earth is simply the keeper of nutrients, a position where historically the plant roots reside and a support base for the development of the plant. The primary purpose of hydroponic growth is to enable plant roots to come into direct contact with the nutrient solution while having access to oxygen as well.

There are many and varied crops produced today using the hydroponic method. These can be classified as follows:

• vegetables like tomatoes, cucumbers, lettuces, cherry, bell peppers.

• Berries and a host of minor ones such as radish, melon, and strawberry

• cut flowers e.g. roses, and carnations

• potted flowers e.g. geraniums, azalea, poinsettia, tulips

• numerous bedding plants

Hydroponics means the cultivation of plants in water. The water is enriched with nutrients. This allows very efficient and sustainable production of high-quality vegetables as well as high-quality fruits and herbs. Hydroponics has a long history. Today, hydroponic plant breeding is seen as a future problem solver for the global food crisis caused by the increasing world population and climate change. Hydroculture is nothing more than plants without soil. The plants grow exclusively in expanded clay. These are these globules that are created by burning the clay at 1200 degrees and then bloating it. Expanded clay does not store water or nutrients. Inside are only air and sound. The plants grow from the beginning in expanded clay. Although it is possible to transplant soil plants into hydroponic plants, it is usually not practicable because the plants need a long time to get used to, and success is not guaranteed.

Hydroculture means that the plant wholly cleaned from the soil is planted in a watertight vessel having a water level indicator with a substrate such as expanded clay. The watertight vessel is necessary because the whole time, there is water with a nutrient solution for the plants in the pot, about which the water level indicator permanently provides information. The most common substrate is currently expanded clay beads made from baked clay. These are also known under the brand name "lecaton" but other substrates, such as perlite, basalt, mineral wool, gravel, sand, and also polystyrene flakes are suitable for hydroponics.

Soilless cultivation of plants in inorganic substrates is known to many hobby gardeners. Hydroculture is the broader sense, which means that plants are cultivated in the water. However, more narrowly stated, it is a system that allows plant growth without the use of potting soil or soil. Hydroculture is very popular amongst private gardeners because of the many benefits it offers. Especially with plant friends who manage in a small space or without a garden, perfect results can be achieved with hydroponics. Typical advantages of hydroponic culture are that no weeds have to be removed, no pests in the soil have to be combated, and that the sensitivity to stress and thus diseases are often reduced. Therefore, plants that grow in hydroponic plants are healthier, grow faster, and flower more quickly, and eventually produce fruit. Another advantage is that through specific extensions, a hydroponic system can also be supplied

semi-automatically or fully automatically with water and nutrients. It is therefore also suitable for those

The care of the original hydroponic culture is facilitated conditionally by the system. The water level gauge usually has three levels, minimum, optimum, and maximum, to ensure optimal, plant-specific care. Of course, as in normal houseplants, the watering intervals of hydro plants vary depending on the pitch, the pot size, and the plant itself. The cleaning of plants, removing dead leaves or parts of plants, and the regular pruning and control of animal and fungal infestation should be regular, respectively.

What plants need to grow healthy?

Plants can evidently build up almost out of nowhere. A bit of water, light, air, and earth seem to be enough to make a small seed to grow a whole shrub. Using carbon from the air, they use the sun's energy to make glucose, which they use to fuel their growth and cell buildup. In fact, plants are so-called autotrophic organisms, i.e. They produce their own food. Of course, they cannot arise out of anywhere. Complex conditions and their precise coordination are necessary to guarantee stable, healthy growth.

Light: energy that gets everything going

Light could almost be described as the most crucial growth factor. It splits the water molecules so that the further process can be triggered, and photosynthesis is started. Too little light

leads to the so-called geilwuchs, whereby root development and leaf growth are neglected in favor of the growth of length so that the plant can get better at a light source. This makes sense when other larger plants cover the smaller one. However, if there is too little light at all, for example, in the interior, the plant can logically still be so long and will not get a photon.

In addition, one can observe in plant growth that they always stretch to the sun. The shadow side of a plant grows faster and faster, so that it inclines towards the sun, to get a maximum of radiation. But not only the direction, but also the nature of the light changes the growth of the plant. Depending on the intensity and wavelengths, different substances form, or the plant generally grows more or less well.

To ensure this environmental factor, you can use artificial light in the form of led plant light, which covers all the wavelengths required for growth and promise better results than purely monochrome light.

Air: carbon dioxide as a base

The carbon dioxide that the plant needs for its construction, it gets from the air. There plant finds, namely, aside from all other gases, carbon dioxide (co2). Inorganic co2 is used to produce important organic compounds that act as building material and energy sources for different parts of the ecosystem.

For example, our vegetable diet serves us as an energy source because the plants process the carbon from the air.

Minerals, nitrogen and other nutrients

The nutrient solution in the hydroponic system is probably the most important factor for success or failure. Unlike fertilizers for garden soils or potting soil, hydroponics requires all nutrient elements. In addition to the known primary nutrients nitrogen, phosphorus, and potassium, these also include magnesium, iron, and trace nutrients such as boron, manganese, and zinc. In addition to the usual liquid fertilizers, various long-term fertilizers are available, which ensure the supply for up to four months. Commercially available fertilizers, which are often cheaper than pure hydroponic fertilizers, also work well. However, the user should be experienced in handling fertilizers. The result of wrong feeding can be salinisation or overdosage.

Having arrived at the nutrients the plant needs for healthy growth, we enter into phytotrophology. A complex term that, in principle, means nothing other than the nutritional science of the plant (phyton means plant and trophology means nutrition). In principle, plants are autotrophic organisms. They can virtually produce their own food.

They do this in photosynthesis, where they produce glucose and oxygen from carbon dioxide and water by supplying energy in the form of light. With this glucose, they get their processes going so that cells can be built up. They also need nutrients from the soil that they absorb through the roots.

Chapter 1: Introduction To Container Gardening!

Container gardening is most suitable and apt for all those with limited ground space. Most people believe that in order to practice gardening, ample yard space is mandatory. This is however not entirely true. You can still work on enhancing your gardening skills and also flaunt a perfectly nurtured garden area if you adapt the concept of container gardening. This eBook will offer useful suggestions in achieving the best garden space all on your own.

Container gardening is the practice of growing produce, plants, vegetables or just anything in a container. As the self-explanatory term advices, you do not need a ground space to do this. All you need is reliable containers, preferably fancy or pretty ones that can add some oomph factor to your all new and sparkling garden area. The best part about container gardening is that you can choose your own spot where you wish to plan a garden. It can be anywhere, even in a tiny corner of your porch or your balcony, rooftop or even a window still, as the only mandatory thing is a good dose of sunlight to help your saplings grow stronger and healthier with the passage of time. It is the best choice for all those residing in apartments and similar urban based locations.

Initially, container gardening was practiced in pots, especially those made exclusively out of terracotta. With the passage of time, these pots have been replaced by plastic ones and window boxes that fit perfectly in any tiny corner of your house. It is ideally used for ornamental purposes where people delighted in the idea of creating a small space but successful garden with eye catching flowers to greet all their visitors. However, it is not restricted to the purpose of beauty alone. Container gardening also encourages the growth of edibles in the form of fresh greens and vegetables that can be consumed for good health and wellbeing. It is also a good practice among people of certain geographical areas where the soil is compromised or unable to offer enough nutrition and scope for the plants to grow. In such cases, a container pot with suitably collected soil makes gardening possible and successful.

Flexibility is a great advantage for all those interested in container gardening. You can choose your own container; it can be anything from mugs, tea cups, pots, fancy boxes or just anything that catches your attention. However, care must be taken while choose a suitable container as it should offer scope for irrigation and drainage which will enable the roots to breathe, absorb nutrition and grow respectively. Container gardening is a great option for beginners who are still finding their way through all the basics of growing and maintaining plants. Another great advantage is that it offers freedom to move your garden wherever and whenever as you see fit. It is not restricted to a particular place as such which makes it a highly flexible option. If you have some space and some idle containers, allow your imagination, creativity and determination to run wild and free for some mind boggling results.

Chapter 2: Preparing For Your Square Foot Garden

You have to decide where you are going to set up your garden and what type of setup are you going to go with that is best suited to your needs. I believe a good choice for a new gardener that is easy to maintain is an elevated boxed or square foot garden. If this is your choice you should have some kind of fencing around to help deter the critters including family pets as you don't want them pooping on your new organic garden. Even though we use other animal manure as organic matter to help feed the garden soil domestic pet do-do is not on the list. When I built my own boxed garden last year my husband and I put up a fence around it to keep our beloved dog (Zowie) out of our garden. We just surrounded it with 8-2×4's on their ends standing up, then nailed them to the garden box frame and surrounded the bottom with chicken wire. We cut another two- 2×4's down to make a gate. It is a simple design but it does the trick. We also installed lattice sheets between the posts so that my morning glories, sunflowers, and beans could grow up them. Of course how much wood you will need will depend on how big your garden box is going to be. Our garden ended up being 20 ft. long and eight feet wide.

Building a Square Foot Garden.

If you have any leftover wood from a previous project you could use it to build the frame of your garden. The wood I used for my garden project was wood left over from a fence we built the previous year. You should choose a spot for your garden where it is protected from the elements such as wind and frost. Also, make sure it is in a spot where it will receive plenty of sunshine with easy water access. If you can install it close to your kitchen it makes it easier for you to run out and get some herbs, and veggies for your meals. My own garden is actually installed on the other end of my house, but it is worth the little walk knowing that I am getting fresh organic vegetables for my family to enjoy. For the box, use two by six pressure treated wooden planks.

Reinforce the planks by putting heavy gauge hinges in the corners. The sides of your frame should be twelve inch deep. Spread some newspaper at the bottom or cardboard to help suppress weeds from growing there. I collected newspapers ahead of time when I built my garden. Put your frame in your chosen spot and then fill the frame with soil. You now have a garden that is waiting to be planted. Finding out what type of produce grows best in your area is something you should check out. Ask around your area to find out what should be planted earlier in the season and what should be planted later in the season. These are things you will need to learn if you truly want to become a true green thumb home gardener!

Feeding Your Soil.

Feed your soil before you do any planting. Feed your soil through mixing in organic matter such as compost, animal manure, and shredded leaves. Fertilizers and Minerals such as rock phosphate and agricultural lime should be added once in a while but the best thing for you to add is organic matter. Using organic matter will help you provide your soil with a source of nutrients and nitrogen which the plants need to grow. Organic matter is also a rich food source for microbes. The organisms make the nutrients available to the plants by carrying out the process of decay.

Making Your Garden Soil Healthy.

When it comes to garden soil most of us are not blessed with the perfect soil for gardening. Don't worry there are things that we can do to improve the health of our soil to ready for gardening. If your soil is too sandy or stony there are steps that you can take to change this once you understand the components that make a soil healthy enough to grow an impressive garden in.

Composition of Your Garden Soil.

Basically Soil is composed of water, air, organic matter, and weathered rock. Signs that are hidden for the most part of a healthy soil are the small animals or organisms, insects, worms and microbes that will flourish when the elements in the soil are in balance. Approximately half of your soil is made up of weathered stone which has been broken down over time by the elements of rain, wind, thawing, freezing, as well as other biological and chemical factors. The type of soil you have is usually judged by the size of the inorganic soil particles. The amount of clay, silt, or sand particles that are in it will determine the texture of your soil. The texture of your soil will affect how well you're soil drains and the amount of nutrients that are available. These factors are going to make a large impact on how your plants in your garden will grow.

Organic Matter in Your Garden.

Organic matter is made up of the partially decomposed remains of plant life and soil organisms. In organic matter you will find such things as trees, mosses, grass, leaves, and other vegetative matter. Organic matter is an important part of your soil even though it only makes up five to 10% of your soil it is a very essential part in creating healthy gardening soil. Organic matter is also a great food source for your garden soil life such as microorganisms. Increase organic matter in your soil by adding mulches, peat moss, compost, green manures. The majority of roots of plants are found in the top six inches of soil so you should concentrate on this part of your garden soil, this will provide your garden with healthy soil.

Soil organisms such as protozoa, earthworms, bacteria, and nematodes are all very important in helping the plants in your garden to grow and stay healthy. Soil organisms convert organic matter into vitamins, disease suppressing compounds, hormones and nutrients all of which plants need to grow. Your garden soil will be bound together by the excretions of soil organisms. Making sure that you provide them with ideal conditions for the organisms to do their work will help ensure that your garden will be healthy.

Making sure to provide the organisms with plenty of food will help keep your garden healthy. The best choice would be organic matter. Aerate your garden soil and provide it with water, but not too much. Aerating the soil it will help in being a source of atmospheric nitrogen that your plants will make use of. Try to cover your garden soil with organic matter and remember to watch that you are not stepping on your plants and never work the soil when it is wet.

Divide Box into Sections.

You can divide your garden box into four one foot sections using tacks and string you can make a grid dividing the box up running the strings in a parallel pattern across your garden box. In each one foot space plant a different vegetable or herb that suits your tastes and will grow well in your geographical location. Try to put the plants that will be the taller ones at the north end so they won't block the light for your smaller garden plants. It may be a good idea only to put one tomato plant in a box as they tend to grow quite large so they need more space. You can train them by putting bamboo poles in and string them up to the pole so they will grow upwards. Smaller plants such as herbs you will be able to put quite a few in one square of your garden box.

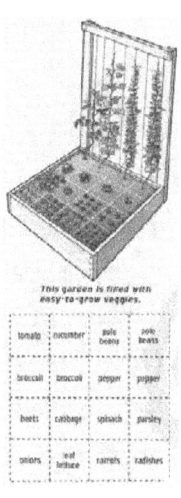

You can remove the grid string, once you have your garden planted. Once your garden begins to fill out the different plants from the different squares will intertwine with one another. They will make a lovely quilt like affect that you will find is very pleasing to the eye. Make sure that you read the instructions on individual plant seed packs, check the instructions to see how much space is needed for the seeds you are planting.

You need to thin out your garden seedlings to avoid overcrowding.

If you are trying your hand at growing a garden for the first time the square foot garden is a good choice. It is relatively small so it won't overwhelm you. You should be able to maintain it with relative ease. With this size of garden you will be able to utilize most or all of the space for growing vegetables and herbs. You will find this to be a great way to introduce yourself into the world of gardening—starting with a square foot garden. Taking this approach will enable you to expand your garden if and when you are ready. If and when this time comes you can just make another box and continue with your square foot gardening techniques.

The square foot gardening is a great set up if you have pets this will separate their part of the yard to use from your garden. Putting some wire fencing such as chicken wire around the border of the garden will help encourage your pets from staying out of the garden. We must try to keep our pets from doing their poops in the garden as well as making sure they are not in there digging up the garden. I know my own dog has a great love for digging holes to bury her bones this was another reason that I put a fence around my own square foot garden to keep my dog's poop and bones out. It is my little piece of green paradise the rest is the dogs, but this little part is for me to enjoy.

Water Barrel.

Investing in a water barrel is a good idea to help lower costs in the water to your garden. You can save money on your water bill by using rain water to provide the water supply for your garden. Try to set up your barrel close to your garden giving you easy access to your water supply. A screen on your water barrel is important in keeping out mosquitoes as they are attracted to stagnant water which they lay their eggs on. Make sure you have a screen on your barrel so you won't be eaten alive while trying to water your special box garden! Using rain water is a great way for you to make use of the natural resources. The rain water can help keep your square foot garden growing, at the same time being a process that is environmentally friendly. Once you become more comfortable with gardening you can start to expand your area of operations. You should think about getting a composter this would be a great way for you to supply your garden with organic matter to feed the soil and plants. For your first shot at gardening you can buy some compost at local gardening supply stores. They can supply you with what you need to get your garden up and growing in a healthy fashion.

Chapter 3: Choosing The Right Medium

Instead of using soil for growing the plants, in hydroponics you will be using a growing medium.

When you are developing your hydroponic system for your hydroponic garden, you will have to consider the kind of medium that you would want to use, the yield that you want to be able to produce and the easiest way to maintain it as well.

In this chapter we will take a look at some of the most common and popular mediums used for hydroponics, the advantages as well as the disadvantages.

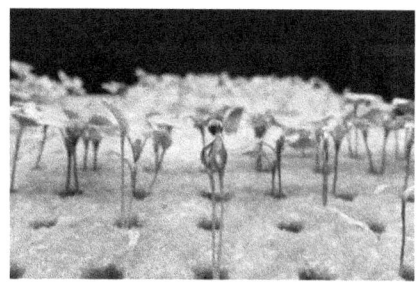

Rockwool is the most commonly used medium in modern hydroponic systems. This material is made from basalt rock and it is melted and later spun so that this material is transformed into strands of fibers that are interconnected.

One of the main advantages of using Rockwool is that it tends to hold onto water well and this means that the chances of your plants becoming dehydrated are reduced. Even in case of the breakdown of the pump, your plants won't be harmed. It not only can retain water, but it also holds onto a lot of air, this means that your plants won't be over watered and they will be aerated as well.

The disadvantages of using this particular medium are the dust and fibers given off by this medium can be harmful, so you will need to be really careful while you are handling it. The pH level of this medium is high as well, this means that you will need to pay extra attention to the nutrient solution that you are using to ensure that the pH level stays balanced, if not your crops might just die.

Coconut fiber is also referred to as coco and this is obtained from the powdered husks of the coconuts. It is gaining popularity because this is a fully organic medium and it can be used in any of the hydroponics systems. This can retain lot of water and oxygen; this means that your plants will have a better chance of staying alive even if something does go wrong with the hydroponics system.

However, you need to be careful about where you are getting your coconut fiber from, because the cheaper varieties tend to contain a lot of sea salt and this can hurt your crops.

Perlite is a form of volcanic glass and it is one of the most affordable mediums that you can get your hands on. This is generally mixed in with other materials because of its price. Due to the wicking action that it performs, Perlite often is used in the wick hydroponic systems.

Perlite cannot retain much water and it can be harmful when ingested. Therefore, you will need to wear dust masks while you are handling it.

Expanded clay pebbles are created by simply baking the clay in a kiln and this creates clay pellets that are filled with air. These clay pellets are comparatively more expensive than the other media that you can use in your hydroponics system.

These expanded clay pebbles are reusable. But they can't retain either oxygen or water well and therefore it is necessary to mix them with other medium for increasing their capacity of retaining water.

Air can be used as a medium as well and when you use air, as a medium it is referred to as no medium and this method is very cost effective because you don't have to technically buy any medium as such.

Since the roots of the crops will be exposed all the time, you will know that they are getting a constant supply of oxygen. But you will need to ensure that there won't be much room for error when you are using air as a growing medium. This means that your roots are at the risk of drying out even if the pump fails for a few minutes and this can cause some serious damage and stoppage of supply of water for a prolonged period of time might kill the entire crop as well.

Chapter 4: Land & The Landscape

When starting your kitchen garden, the first thing that you will need is an appropriate area. The perfect area will be one that receives about 6 hours of ample sunshine every day. This can be in your backyard, patio, terrace or even by a large, open window.

So as you have finalized your plan to grow your own food, take a good critical look around your residence. Is there any location that fits the sunshine requirement? If yes, then that is going to be the spot for your small kitchen garden.

Ideally, an open space like the front veranda or back yard or even terrace would be perfect but if you live in a small space, indoors can work too. Though they can be a little tricky to handle. Outdoors are preferable because the mess is easily managed and drainage is easier.

If you have a large back yard or front lawn, then naturally you have nothing to worry about. However, you can still plant even if you live in a small space or have no access to ground. The best way to go around it is to have a raised bed. You can easily construct it and it is very space efficient. Never heard of the raised bed? Do not worry! That is why you have this book.

Raised Bed & Square Foot Gardening

Traditionally crops are grown in long rows. You would have seen it in movies, shows or even when driving along the countryside. The method has been used for centuries and is drainage efficient but is not the most space efficient.

When people start their own garden, they mimic the row style of plantation because that is what they have most commonly seen. However, for small spaces and small home gardens, a square foot method or a raised bed style is much more preferable.

In the simplest of the terms, a raised bed is basically a large sized plantation box. Most raised beds are 4 x 8 sq. ft. or 4 x 6 sq ft. It is efficient because it can be placed anywhere that gets ample sunshine, offers quick drainage and is space saving. You don't need to go out and buy one immediately. You can even build one easily by following the outlined steps.

Building a raised bed

Raised beds come in various designs and materials. The one outlined below is the easiest to make. Naturally, you can use various different materials but wood is the most common. Amongst wood types, cedar is perhaps the best because of its natural resistance. A more experiences gardener can try different woods and materials but as a beginner, I would suggest that you stick to cedar wood and keep the depth at the standard 12 inches. Deeper raised beds are also made but they can be more expensive. This raised bed will be sufficient for most common crops.

Materials

2 Cedar Boards 8 ft. x 12" x 2"
2 Cedar Boards 4 ft. x 12" x 2"
Deck Screws
Drill
Shovel
Pottery Rubble
Soil Mix

Method

Clear a 4 ft. by 8 ft. area in a location that gets ample sunshine. If it is on ground, remove the grass using your shovel.

Align the boards in the shape of a box. Take the help of a friend. On all adjacent corners, make hole markings. Make sure that they align with each other.

Drill the holes into the boards.

One by one secure the boards together with the help of deck screws. Use as many as you need. You need to make sure that the structure stands up sound.

Place the frame on the area you cleared and check the balance. It should be level and should not rock to and fro.

Spread the pottery rubble or small stones at the bottom. This will facilitate drainage.

Fill up to the top with your soil mix.

At the start, you can begin with only one raised bed. Then as you begin to grow more, you can increase the number of raised beds in your kitchen garden.

Dividing into square feet

As mentioned earlier, in this method, the crops are planted in square ft. instead of rows. Once you have built your raised bed, you can then proceed to divide it.

Materials

Marker
Ruler/Measuring Tape
Nails
Hammer
String

Method

Using a board marker and a ruler, mark the horizontal and vertical lengths in 1 ft. increments. So there will be 4 marks horizontally and 8 marks vertically.

Hammer small nails into the marked points.

Tie strings across parallel nails. The strings should be taut and tense.

By the time you are finished, your raised bed should like a grid with each box have an area of 1 sq. ft.

Each square can be used to grow a different crop. So in this particular case, you can have 32 different types (4 x 8 = 32) growing simultaneously!

Further Space Saving Tricks

You can smartly utilize limited space further by keeping in mind the following tips and tricks.

☐ In case of vines and climbers (such as watermelons and peas), encourage them to grow upwards be providing adequate support. Do not let them sprawl across the ground. This will be messy and will take too much space. You can even wrap them around a pillar, a lamp post or a swing. Or you can vertically erect a lumber post. Some vines will even wrap around a taut string.

☐ Plant breeders have now developed dwarf varieties of their larger cousins. These are small in size but yield the same vegetable/fruit. Great when you have limited space.

☐ Make sure that you are rotating crops. Growing the same crops in the same place over and over depletes the soil. With square foot gardening, you can grow tomatoes in one square one year and in another the next year. This will not drain the soil as much. Keep your garden varied.

☐ Container gardening can be your best friend. One of my friends grows parsley in small pots that she keeps on her kitchen window. The parsley is thriving and it is easy
to pick it up when you need it in cooking. Your kitchen garden should not be restricted to one place. You can have it sprawled all around the house.

The Soil Mix

Soil is the nurturing source for your plants. It is from the soil that your plants will draw their moisture and all necessary nutrients. A poor soil mix will result in poor plant growth. In an ideal world, the soil conditions should vary according to the crop being grown. However, realistically nobody has the time or resources to do that. Hence a general soil makeup that benefits most varieties is usually perfect.

To the untrained eye, soil is just soil. However, the gardener knows that there are many types and the composition of different ingredients can drastically affect crop yield. Ideally, garden soil should contain equal parts of clay, sand and silt. You cannot know for certain the composition of your own household soil unless you get it tested from a laboratory. It can be expensive. If you are gardening using a raised bed, I would suggest purchasing pre-made soil mix. Initial starter soil mixes are also available. Check out your local gardening shop. They are not that expensive and can act as a great starting base.

The ideal soil mix should also contain about 5% organic matter. You can mix it when laying the soil or you can buy a soil mix that already contains the adequate amount.

For good gardening, you also need to **aerate the soil** at least once or twice a year. Fortunately, doing that is very easy. Just follow the given steps.

Using a space, dig a 6" deep hole at one side of your raised bed.

Dig a similar hold about two feet away from it.

Fill the first hole with the dug up soil of the second hole.

Continue doing this for the entire length of your garden (or raised bed).

It is a good idea to do this before plantation of seeds.

Earthworms are also very good aerators. So if you see them around, let them do their magic. They do wonders for garden soil.

Adjusting Soil pH

The pH of the soil is extremely important for efficient growth. Soil that is too acidic or too alkaline will destroy the plants. I highly recommend that you purchase a soil pH meter. They are not very expensive and can really come in handy. You can get one from here.

Ideally the pH of the soil should be between 6 and 7. If your soil is too alkaline (the pH number is high), you will need to treat it be mixing in some sulphur or aluminum sulphate. If it is too acidic, you will need to mix in limestone.

Always do the pH testing and treatment before you begin planting.

Some rare varieties (for example blueberries) prefer more extreme pH (more acidic for blueberries). If you plan on growing them, I would suggest that you use a container. That way, you won't have to alter the pH of your whole soil mix.

Fertilizers

Undoubtedly the most misunderstood aspect of gardening. Most people think that the more they fertilize the soil, the better it will be for the plants, right? Wrong! Too much fertilization can actually harm your plants.

For organic gardening, I do not recommend commercial synthetic fertilizers. Instead natural compost is the best way to go. It doesn't even take that much effort. Everything you need for your compost pile, you probably already have it.

Building a compost pile

Materials

3 ft. Wide Tin Sheet
Welding Equipment

Method

Roll the tin sheet so that it has a 2-3 ft. diameter.

Get it welded across the edges so that you have a hollow cylinder with no base.

Place it in a shaded place, preferably under a tree. The place should have good drainage. Keep in mind that it should be slightly away from your house as the compost pile will smell.

Put all sorts of organic waste into your compost pile. This can include rotten vegetables, onion skins, potato skins, fallen leaves, old twigs and even stale bread and such. Just do not add meat of any kind.

Turn the pile every few weeks or so.

Slowly over time, all of this will naturally decompose and become one giant pile of rich, smelly soil like material. This is all the fertilizer that you need.

Ideally, fertilization should be done twice in a season. Once, before the seeds are sown and then fertilizing during mid growth. For first type, you will mix the compost with the soil. For the second type, a technique called **side dressing** is used. For that, you dig a narrow hole adjacent (about 6" away) to the plants roots and fill it with compost. Then cover it up with soil. As you will water, the nutrients will leech out and nourish the plant roots.

Chapter 5: Fruits

In terrace gardening, the most satisfying and thrilling moment is when one sees fruits on the plants. In my garden I have planted fruit trees which do not need too much care and attention and they are planted in 2 feet by 2 feet containers. Many fruit trees like avocado, guava; pomegranate and orange to name a few, can be successfully grown on the terrace in containers and sun light can be fully made use of. Containers can be moved as per need and insect attacks can be controlled easily.

Guava

Guavas come in various shapes and sizes and the trees look beautiful with white flowers with mild fragrance. They grow in tropical and semi-tropical climate and a grafted plant gives fruit in about 2 years. The plant we have is about 3 feet and is giving fruit since last two years.

Lemon

A grafted lemon plant purchased from a nursery, planted in a 2 feet by 2 feet pot started giving fruits in 2 years. Plants from seeds take 8 to10 years to yield fruits and grow very big in size which is not suitable for a container. This small plant produces lemon through- out the year and when the numbers are more we use them in making pickles and juice. Some of the recipes are available in this book. The fragrant leaves can be used as flavouring agent in recipes like curd-rice (Dahi-bhat).

Orange

Orange trees, the grafted ones, are easy to grow in pots. The fragrant smell of white flowers and the glossy deep green foliage, even during summer months, are a pleasure to watch. We have planted a grafted plant and it started giving fruits in the second year. Every 2 to 3 years the plant needs to be re-potted to a bigger pot to allow further growth. The fruits require more than 8 months to mature and ripeness can be determined when the fruits change colour from deep green to yellow-orange depending on the variety.

The plant needs to be placed in a sunny spot and need more water when flowering and forming small fruits.

Pomegranate

Pomegranates trees are the best suited to grow in containers. The fruits get ready in 4-5 months and the tree starts giving fruits in two years. Initially the fruits fall off, but if pruned to a single stick with 2-3 branches, the fruits start developing. It is a bushy plant with bright red-orange flowers and it is fascinating to watch the development of fruits. We have about 20 fruits in different stages in the plant at the time of writing this book and the bush is 5 feet tall.

Pineapple

Pineapples can be grown in containers very easily but it takes two years to give a fruit. A ripe pineapple cut from the leaf side can be planted; it takes roots and becomes a new plant

Mango

Mangoes, known as the king of the fruits in India, are natives to Asian countries. They are tropical trees and now- a -days are available in dwarf varieties which is why they can be planted in containers. The plant we have is only one year old at the time of writing this book and we will have to wait for two more years for the pleasure of having fruits on this tree.

Avocado

This grafted plant on the terrace is 2-3 feet tall, and looks healthy and bushy. It is 3 years old.

Chapter 7: Perennial Vegetables

Perennial vegetables are vegetables that can live and produce a harvestable yield for at least 2 years without needing to be replanted. This means that after a perennial plant reaches maturity and bears a crop, it will grow back on its own the following year, allowing you to get the most from your garden with as little amount of work as possible.

In this book, you'll find out which vegetables are perennials and can be easily grown in your backyard garden. Note that not all plants are the same and each one may require a different environment in order to thrive. Make sure you check and see if your chosen plants will get along with your local climate. This chapter will discuss the different preparations you'll need to make that will generally be the same for all plants, regardless of what you choose.

Garden Beds

A backyard garden is often considered the best place to start planting perennial vegetables. Opt for a raised garden bed since they tend to yield better crops, and they also make it easier to tend to your plants. Try to create one large bed, at least 5 feet wide and as long as you can make it. Just make sure that the width of the vegetable bed is wide enough that you can easily water all the plants, even those at the center. The height of the raised bed should be at least 6 inches – this is perfect for rooting plants and makes it easy for you to care for your plants.

There are several ways you can "raise" the bed, starting with simply digging a trench to define the plot. Other homeowners prefer to create a box and simply filling it with their chosen soil. The latter is usually better since you don't have to deal with erosion, plus the vegetable bed is completely out of your way with zero chances of stepping on it.

The beauty of raised beds is that you'll be giving your plants loose soil to begin with – making it easier for them to grow. The vegetables also bunch up together so there's little space for weeds. If you don't think you have the space for a proper plot, you can also try using pots, bags, or even hanging baskets to raise your perennial vegetables. Later on in this book, you'll find out exactly how this can be done.

Soil Mixes

The soil is the next most important thing when it comes to growing perennial vegetables. The soil in your backyard may not be good enough to produce high-quality fruits and vegetables. Most vegetables thrive best in loose soil with a pH of around 6.5. You can try testing your own soil to see if you meet these requirements. Buying ready made garden soil is also a good idea if you want to reduce the work process. There are

many types of high-quality soil available from your local garden supply store that are already at the proper pH.

Pros and Cons of Perennials

The pros of growing perennials definitely outweigh the cons, but that doesn't mean that there aren't things that can go wrong. By being aware of potential problems before you experience them, you'll have the chance to at least prepare a system that will let you avoid them.

Pros

After the initial investment of time, perennial vegetables will grow back almost automatically, year after year.

They are known for being hardy and tough. This is a plus for inexperienced gardeners, who are bound to make some mistakes while learning the basics.

These plants often have several uses. In addition to providing edible vegetables, many perennial plants also work well as decorations.

There's an incredible variety available. The world of perennial plants extends far beyond the vegetable realm and includes fruit bearing trees and berry bushes.

Many types grow well indoors as well as out.

Cons

Some perennials may take a long time before they become useful or start bearing anything edible.

Perennials are pretty much capable of taking care of themselves, but if you leave them alone for long, there's a good chance that they'd take over the garden. Growing up so fast, some perennials may start to spread all over the place, killing other plants. They have a tendency to become invasive, so you'll want to keep an eye on them.

Since these plants are planted for the long haul, it's important to plant these perennials somewhere permanent or a place where you won't have to move them again.

They can be more vulnerable to diseases since you're not using crop rotation, which naturally prevents disease among plants.

What Perennial Vegetables are Worth Growing?

The following chapters will provide information about different perennial vegetables that you can grow in your garden, as well as what you can do to help them thrive. Note that not all vegetables are the same and the requirements for raising them will vary. It's usually best to combine vegetables that will thrive under the same conditions, and we'll talk a little more about how to go about doing that as we go along.

Chapter 8: Gardening Can Be Easy

My objective was to make this book very easy and basic to follow as I said in my introduction. If you live in an apartment building, two things should be considered other than just where the sun light hits the balcony and for how long it stays on the balcony. It would be wise to check with the apartment manager or body corporate before you start. Also, if you are positioned above a very busy road, it would be worthwhile checking if the fallout from car fumes will make it less healthy for you to grow your own vegetables. This is just a note of precaution but in this fast moving world, sometimes, we need to consider things that in a previous time we may not have needed to even think in passing about. The other area I would be looking at is whether you have good drainage on the balcony you intend to grow plants. Obviously there will be run off when you are watering your plants and your downstairs neighbors will probably not appreciate water cascading onto their balcony. Again, in the interest of neighborly relationships, it's worth while checking this out. There is a way to overcome run off issues and that is simply have a large plastic container under the area that you are watering. Let the container collect the excess water and re use it on the plants the next time you water with a spare container to collect that lot of excess water.

Once you have the set up of your new garden under control and done, the basic maintenance such as watering and putting a good organic fertilizer on it should be very quick and easy. A check for any unwanted dinner guest to your vegetables, again, should be a quick job. In fact, some times the evidence of these pests will be starring you in the face. I personally hold no mercy for these critters and head straight away for an organic spray or powder to remedy the situation. I do, however, take great care not to use remedies when my good bugs, such as, lady bugs or bees are active during the day. Even if you are growing your fruit and vegetables on high rise apartment building balconies, chances are the bad bugs will find them. After dealing with the bad boys you can look forward to eating the fruits that your labors will give out. I can assure you that the hardest part will be testing out new recipes to use your delicious results and really, that will translate into a joy rather than a chore. There really is nothing like the feeling of popping down or out to your own garden to pick fresh ingredients for your favorite recipe. Don't be surprised when using the freshest possible ingredients your favorite recipe just got whole lot better.

If you follow the steps in this book as to the set up of your garden and a few tools to make your life a little safer and easier, you will be able to sit and admire the new life that you have created around you in no time at all. Not to mention the absolute health benefits that comes from eating highly nutritious, fresh fruit and vegetables.

Chapter 9: Perennial Fruit Bearing Trees And Bushes

Many of the fruit bearing perennial plants are trees, bushes or shrubs. All of the berries we will be exploring are bushes or shrubs. The examples are well known and widely used varieties of perennial berries and, no matter where you live, growing one or two of them should be both possible and worthwhile.

Blueberries (Vaccinium corymbosum)

The blueberry bush is native to North America and wasn't introduced to the European diet until well into the twentieth century. These versatile and delicious berries grow on bushes that can vary in size from six inches to nearly thirteen feet. The blueberry can be enjoyed in pies, smoothies, on top of cereals and ice cream or enjoyed as soon as they are picked from the bush.

Blueberries can be grown from seed, but expect to wait five years or so before you can harvest anything worthwhile. An easier solution is to purchase a young bush from a local nursery and transplant it to your garden.

The plant does best in soil with a pH that ranges from 4.0-5.5 and prefers a sunny spot. Peat moss is a good choice for planting blueberries in. They should be ready to harvest midway through their growing season.

Nutritionally, blueberries are being hailed as a superfood because of their high concentrates of anthocyanins, polyphenols, and several phytochemicals.

These compounds are considered potentially very useful to the human body, and they are constantly being studied so that their effects and benefits can be better understood.

Even without the alleged super compounds mentioned above, blueberries have a lot of good things going for them. They are high in Omega Three acids, Phosphorus, and Potassium. Vitamin wise blueberries are a decent source of B complex, A and K.

Blackberries (Rubus fruticosus)

Blackberries grow in thorny bushes known as "brambles".

They are popular as a pie filling and also enjoyed raw.

Blackberry bushes grow well in sandy, well-drained, acidic soil and full sunlight. The roots are susceptible to rotting if they are too damp, so make sure that they are always well drained. Planting on a hill or slope helps out here. Expect to wait two years before the berries are ready to be harvested.

They are a good source of Vitamin A and dietary fiber.

It is worth noting that Blackberries or Raspberries thrive in soil that was previously used to grow Nightshades.

Raspberries (Rubus idaeus)

Raspberries are very similar to Blackberries and are closely related. They also grow on thorny bushes and share soil and sunlight preferences.

Raspberries may have a different taste than blackberries, but when it comes to growing them, they are pretty identical.

Goose Berries (Ribes uva-crispa)

Before you consider growing Gooseberries, check and make sure they are legal in your state. Goose Berries are commonly afflicted with White Pine Blister Rust and are forbidden in states where there are a large number of White Pine trees.

If you are permitted to grow one, make sure you have the proper amount of space, these bushes can reach heights of five feet and be just as wide!

Gooseberries are popular in jams, jellies, and preserves. Gooseberries are also used to make tea, as a flavoring for soft drinks and sometimes made into wine.

There are several different varieties available and all of them taste different, so be sure to do some research first, to find one that you like best.

Plant these in a high sunlight area and use well-drained soil. You should be able to harvest some berries after the second year, but waiting until the fourth or fifth year will tend to produce a better tasting berry.

Gooseberries are a good source of Pantothenic Acid, Vitamin C, and fiber. By the way- no one is really sure why they are called "Goose Berries." Geese don't really like them.

Strawberries (Fragaria ananassa)

Strawberries are universally loved by people everywhere. Juicy and delicious, the strawberry is hard to beat. Love of them reaches back to ancient Rome, and they were harvested in parts of Europe as early as the fourteenth century. By the 1500's, the Strawberry was being cultivated and enjoyed throughout most of the European Continent.

Raw, dusted with sugar, frozen and blended, baked into pies, squeezed into juices- there are so many ways to enjoy them, it's impossible to pick just one.

Strawberries tend to grow easily and will do well in most areas. They prefer acidic soil and full-on sunlight.

Remember that just about everyone loves to eat these wonderful berries! You may want to consider growing them indoors in hanging baskets, in order to minimize the number of birds, animals and insects that are unable or unwilling to resist such a temptation.

Not nearly a nutritional powerhouse like other berries, Strawberries are still a good source of Vitamin C and some fiber.

While these next two examples are not technically berries, I wanted to mention them because they are popular examples of perennial fruits, offer a relatively large return on a small investment of time and money and they also pair well with any of the berries listed above.

Apples are mentioned because they are often used in similar ways to berries. Both are frequently baked into pies, eaten raw, added to salads, juiced and preserved as jams and jellies.

Grapes make the list for many of the same reasons. Planting an apple tree, a grape vine, a raspberry bush or two and some strawberries would provide a nice variety of homegrown fruits that can be used in a variety of ways and enjoyed for years to come.

Grapes (Vitis vinifera)

Grapes have been cultivated by humans for thousands of years and harvested from the wild since the Neolithic period. Yeast, which is necessary for fermentation, naturally occurs on the skin of the grape. This makes it an ideal choice for making wine and other alcoholic drinks. This ability to facilitate fermentation is why grapes were grown by early people in the first place.

The uses for grapes go far beyond wine and brandy production. They are also popular as a juice and often eaten raw as well as being dried into raisins.

Grapes grow on vines that can live and produce fruit for upwards of fifty years or so. Grow them in full sun, along the south side of your property. You can grow them in clay pots to save space.

Table grapes are commonly eaten right off the vine, whereas wine grapes tend to be seedier and are better for juicing or fermenting. Both table and wine grapes come in red and white varieties.

Their are several kinds of grapes that work well in home gardens. Which ones will depend on your local climate.

Grapes contain a decent about of B complex Vitamins and are a good source of Vitamin K.

Apples (Malus domestica)

An apple tree is a fine addition to just about any backyard able to accommodate one. The best thing to do, if you're interested in your own apple tree is to visit a local orchard to see which varieties do well in your area. You may also want to purchase a sapling, since growing a tree from seed will take more time than most would want to wait.

Apples are not native to North America but were brought here in the 1600's by European settlers and the first apple Orchard was planted in 1625. Apples have a long history of human use and may have even been the first tree to be cultivated by people thousands and thousands of years ago.

Most people eat apples raw but they are also good baked and are commonly used in pies and other desserts as well as juices, ciders and vinegar. Culinary uses for apples are nearly limitless, making them a good choice for a back yard garden.

Apples are a healthy alternative to common snack foods and pack a quite a nutritional punch. High in fibers and a decent source of trace minerals, the apple is a solid choice for your garden.

Aside from the fruits and berries mentioned above, the perennial family also contains many useful herbs that are also simple to grow and care for. In the next chapter, we'll take a look at some of them and what they have to offer you.

Chapter 10: Understanding Plants

Understanding the types of plants will help you decide which plant you wish to grow in your gardens. Hence, it is the first and foremost chapter. You need to understand the significance of each type of plant listed below and make your choices accordingly! So, let us start with the first lesson.

Annuals

The life plan of annuals is one year. They germinate, grow, flower and die all in a span of one year. But one advantage of annuals is that they are bold. The disadvantage being, they die quick. Examples are corn, wheat, rice, beans and watermelons.

Peas

Biennials

The life span of biennials is also short. They live for about two years by spreading out their time- growing in the first year and flowering in the second. Biennial are also colorful flowering plants, similar to annuals. For example- onion, cabbage, parsley, silverbeet, and carrot.

Parsley

Perennials

The life span of perennials is more than two years. These are the plants that flower in the spring and summer seasons, every year. They are the ones that stay for a long time. A disadvantage in growing perennials is that they sometimes die during the winter season, but they grow their leaves back in spring. Examples are begonia, coneflower and banana.

Coneflower

Grasses

There are a variety of grasses and each grass type has it own life span. While some are evergreen, others die quick. The most important trick to have a perfect garden is to pick the correct grass. There are cool season grasses like : Kentucky bluegrass, creeping bentgrass, fescue and wheatgrass and there are warn season grasses like : bahiagrass, buffalograss, centipedegrass and bermuda grass. You should be careful while selecting grass and select according to the kind of weather conditions in your area.

Trees

Along the varieties of trees on the planet, the evergreen trees provide color all throughout the year. Whereas the deciduous trees bring green leaves in spring and color in autumn. Trees have very long life spans and are usually planted in garden to achieve enclosure and permanence.

European Larch (deciduous)

Shrubs

Shrubs are like smaller trees with a woody framework instead of a long thick stem. They are also permanent structures with long life spans. Some shrubs are evergreen and some are deciduous, some flower (**andromeda**) while some do not (**bamboo palm**). They form the foundation of any garden because they form the structure and organize the form of the garden.

Andromeda, a flowering shrub

Climbers

There is a variety of climbers and hence different life spans for each. These plants tend to scramble up walls, trellises, boundary walls etc and are planted to soften the hard landscaping by giving the garden an effect of free flow. Many types of climbers have beautiful flowers, and some are scented, for example, **climbing roses, clematis and wisteria**.

Climbing Roses

Aquatics

There is a need to study about aquatics only if you have a pond in your garden. There Is a wide variety of plants in this type too. There are marginals with beautiful flowers that live in shallow water, for example, Zephyr Lily and Chameleon Plant . Moreover, there are spectacular deep-water aquatics, for example Water Lilies.

Water Lilies

Chapter 11: All Methods Of Gardening Share These Same Benefits

Two often unanticipated benefits of gardening are its delightful connection to nature and its remarkable stress-relief side effect.

Connection to Nature

Gardening is really taking your place in nature. You are working with natural elements to bring forth delicious and nutritious produce to be eaten by your own household. After you start gardening, you will feel more in touch with life outside your home. The insects, breeze, rain, and all other elements of Mother Nature will start to become more noticeable to you. You might be out at a friend's house and hear the thunder. Normally, you might think nothing of it.

Since you have been gardening, you might think, "I hope my tomatoes can make it through a storm." Gardening will also allow you to escape the technology of the world. It allows you to stop and smell the roses. You can leave that cell phone in the house and take a short, electronic vacation. If you take the time and dedication, you can enjoy the smells, sounds, and colors of your garden. It generates a reason for you to get off the couch and go outside.

Stress Relief

People often garden for stress relief. It can be very therapeutic. The act of doing the responsibilities gardening requires can relax the mind. It is easy to get outside and enjoy the fresh air. The change in pace can allow your mind to clear and relieve you from the everyday issues we get stuck thinking about.

The pride in the success of a garden can make the work less of a chore and more enjoyable. The physical activity required releases endorphins, which in turn release a lot of tension built up from our everyday lives. You can be getting a large amount of exercise without even realizing it. You will also be getting sunlight, i.e., vitamin D, which is great for your health. It's a free vitamin D day when you garden. Soak up the sunshine and enjoy your new-found passion.

Supplies

If you decide to garden using the straw bale gardening method, you'll need to search out a few supplies. The bales of straw that you purchase can be bought from a farm, feed store or a garden supply store. Purchasing straw from the farm is the best option. It's important that it is straw and not hay. Hay is different and less nutritious. There will also be many types of seeds in hay bales and you will be plagued with grass sprouts.

The best time to purchase straw bales is in the fall. Farmers will have a large supply and be willing to get rid of their bales for less expense. You will not be using the bales until spring, which is fine. Sitting over the winter will not hurt your bales.

You will also need to determine your watering system. You can purchase or craft a drip system. You can also use a sprinkler system. The bales will be held together with twine when you purchase them. Keep the twine in place. This will help you to keep the bales from falling apart.

Position

The first step to gardening with straw bales is to decide where you are going to place your bales. They need to get a lot of sun so avoid placing under trees or areas up against houses. The shade will not let them prepare as they should. You'll want to position everything where it can get at least 4-6 hours of sun.

Lay down landscape fabric or even thick amounts of newspaper. This will help keep pests away and help weeds from growing up through the bales. Position the bales so that the twine is running around each bale. The twine also serves the purpose of holding the bale together as the straw breaks down. This will help to let you know that you have the straw in the right direction.

Now look at the top and bottom of each bale. One will have straw that is bent and the other will have straw that looks like a horrible haircut. Set your bales with the horrible-haircut on top. This will allow the water to drizzle through the straw holes like drizzling water into a drinking straw. If it is in the wrong direction, the water will run right through.

Decomposing Process

The next step is to condition the bales. This is the process that will start to get the decomposing process going. The first 6 days require that you place 3 cups of fertilizer in the bale every other day. The bales should be watered down well every single day. Days 7-9 will require 1 ½ cups of fertilizer. You will still water down the bales well every day. On day 10, you have to add 3 cups of phosphorous and potassium.

During the conditioning process, you might see some black spots. Mushrooms might grow. These are great signs that the microorganisms that you need are present. Exposure to the sun will make the bales heat up to very warm temperatures. If you stick your finger inside a bale you will feel that it is very warm inside. The bales might even steam in the cooler weather. This is how you know you are on the right track. The new plants will love having the higher temps.

Let your bales sit for two days, then insert an old meat thermometer into the middle. If it registers over 105F (40C), it's too hot to plant your seeds or bedding plants. If you don't have an old meat thermometer, wiggle your hand into a bale. If it's too hot, pull your hand out. Water your bales thoroughly for a few days, then check the temp again.

Planting

When your bales temperature is 105F (40C), the bales are ready and you can place some seeds or bedding plants in the bales. There is no real limitation to what you can grow in the bales. Vegetables and fruits that grow very tall should not be planted. It's possible that they will get top heavy and cause the bales to tip over.

For bales in which seeds will be planted, pour a 2-inch thick layer of potting mix all over the top of the straw bale, then read your package instructions to know how deep to plant each specific types of plant seeds. For bedding plants or seedlings, use a trowel or screwdriver to separate the straw and create a pocket to place the bedding plant. Place some planting mix in the hole, then put the bedding plant in afterward.

You can use every exposed side of the bales. Some people have been known to place vegetables and fruit in the top, then plant varieties of herbs on the sides. Some people plant decorative flowers in the sides of the bales that face the back of the house for décor purposes.

The plants will need to be placed according to their spacing instructions. You will want to give them enough room to grow and spread out. Weeds will not be a problem but your plants will fight with each other for space and nutrients if you plant them too closely. McAllen's book details three lists of produce that you can plant in three different bales. You are going to be able to get a lot of plants in one bale if you use all the space provided. You have 5 sides to work with. That is more room than you have with the small rectangular area the bale is taking up.

Straw bale gardening is a perfect medium but is for certain the answer if you have poor soil. It does not require a lot of room, maintenance, or skill. It might not be the best option for everyone, but there are a certain amount of people looking for low maintenance growing of great produce. Plus, even people in wheelchairs can return to gardening. If the bales are still too low, obtain several wooden pallets for each bale and raise them to the desired height.

Chapter 12: The Beauty Of Perennial Vegetables

Anyone can grow a perennial vegetable garden. We can just plant the veggies once, sit down and relax afterward, and then "enjoy the vegetables of our labors" for many years to come. Okay, that was bad, but, believe it or not, perennial vegetables are among the cheapest and healthiest garden produce around. Growing perennial vegetables is also great for those of us who can't really afford to spend large amounts of time on gardening.

Unlike fruits and their abundance, we do not have too many special perennial vegetable varieties. A good portion of them grow in various climates. Once you have established a perennial vegetable garden, you need not maintain it that much, unlike other garden types. Plant them once, and you'll get your harvest year after year.

A Closer Look

Perennial vegetables are all about efficiency and convenience. Coming from certain plants, they are prepared and consumed just like regular vegetables and are known to live for two years or more.

Some popular perennial vegetables that hail from temperate regions all over the world include the artichoke, rhubarb, and asparagus. The taro and cassava varieties are also popular in the tropics; these survivors could last in your garden for many, many years.

Perennial vegetables play an important role in today's cultural diets, especially in tropical areas. It's a different story in Western cultures; once industrial agriculture gained a foothold, nothing could stop it. Many see the practicality factor of Industrial agriculture as the better solution to fast-paced progress. Sorrel, Good King Henry, sea kale, and skirret are good examples of the older temperate varieties that were eventually introduced into the fold.

It must also be noted that perennial vegetables (especially the plants themselves), are integral components of successful forest garden adventures, as these are incorporated into the herbaceous (think of ground cover) or low-growing canopy layers (shrubs/overstory tree types).

Most vegetable plants that we know of are considered annuals – their entire lifespan (from the seeds and all the way to the harvest) cover a couple of months or an entire year. However, depending on the climate, perennial vegetables come back to life every spring. And with proper care, this hardy bunch can produce for a couple of years, and probably more.

Many varieties are also attractive enough that they introduce a healthy variety and interest to gardens. You can exploit this by dedicating a separate space somewhere in your garden. It's an easy undertaking since these vegetable varieties do not need much attention as compared to other traditional annual vegetables.

The following is a comprehensive list of perennial vegetables you could readily try at home: edible hibiscus, perennial leek, potato onion, tree onion/walking onion, udo,
arracacha, breadfruit, asparagus, saltbush, Malabar spinach, sea beet, Good King Henry, tree collards or tree kale, kai-lan, Turkish rocket, camas, achira, aji Amarillo, Manzano Chile, papaya, chicory, chaya, ivy gourd/perennial cucumber, taro, sea kale, artichoke, air

and sweet potato, hyacinth bean, cassava, lotus, oca, runner bean, sorrel, rhubarb, skirret, babaco papaya, and the fragment spring tree (xiangchun).

Annual Agriculture Origins

Perennial vegetable crops are a rarity in North American landscapes and gardens. Aside from asparagus, artichokes, and rhubarb, most gardeners probably do not know the tasty and exceptionally low-maintenance bounty they could readily harvest since many annual crops are not always there.

Most farming and gardening traditions in North American lands are borrowed from Europe, where only a few perennial crops can be found (except for nuts and fruits, of course). A greater portion of the North American landmass is best suited for crops that come from warm, tropical regions, and as it turned out, a lot of perennial vegetables were discovered there.

Some questions remain, like why folks in North America haven't been growing perennial vegetables all these years? Or why not much effort was exerted in domesticating perennials in colder/temperate climates? The origins of agriculture in various civilizations all over the world may have something to do with it, including certain historical peculiarities of the crops grown in certain regions. In tropical regions, particularly in Asia, Latin America, and Africa, agriculture had a strong foundation around starchy and root crop staples. This paved the way for the practice of growing crops together with vines, trees, annuals, and perennials. Agriculture in cold and temperate Eurasia emphasizes more on annual crops such grains and legumes.

Why, or how, did this happen? Logically, it's partly due to the availability of plants in various regions, which were used as raw materials for domestication. With greater diversity, we are presented with more choices for perennial vegetable candidates in the tropics.

Along the way, Europeans notably adopted certain wild edible perennial plants. They bred them together with the usual annual crops (brassica's and beets). The Andean folks, on the other hand, saw fit to domesticate perennial arracacha forms, instead of their annual varieties. In fact, there also appeared many perennial vegetable types all over tropical Americas, such as perennial beans, chaya, and chayote. Since North America does not have domesticated draft animals to pull plows, some experts are convinced this led to the absence of greater perennial vegetable varieties.

It must be noted that back then all farm work was only possible due to the availability of hand tools. This allowed certain areas of any farm from getting the "custom treatment," that is, doing away with the need to invest extra effort and energy. In the Old World "practices," draft animals mainly plow larger areas of a farm. To grow perennials would mean certain areas must be set aside because of differing management approaches. This might explain the concept of "annualizing" perennial wild crops, such as brassica's and beets.

There's another intriguing angle regarding agricultural history. It turned out that the summer-rain-winter Mediterranean drought climate type sparked Eurasian agriculture (which is also a fit for annuals). The crops involved were introduced and adopted northwards in Europe and were thought to have superseded perennial growth and development that would have manifested otherwise.

We must also not forget another factor, where the primary goal of early crop domestication was to get enough food for their survival. It could be that raw materials coming from annuals present quicker rewards than that of perennials, specifically in colder climates where shorter seasons often require some years before perennials begin bearing.

Whatever the case for our neglect in the past was, there can now be no other reason why we should continue ignoring such useful and very productive crops at all. Perennials have the potential to become available at a wide range. And networks of gardeners will have to successfully present them to the world stage as a new and critical component for food production all over North America in the near future.

What We Get From Perennial Vegetables

Grow more food with less sweat – this seems a nice way of putting perennial vegetables into the spotlight. Growing perennial vegetables is easy if you place them side by side with other existing and favored farming concepts, like growing annuals. With it, you can combine effective permaculture gardening techniques with edible landscaping ingenuity for a truly effective gardening system.

New agricultural breakthroughs are announced with promises of higher yields, longer growing seasons, and most of all, less work involved. Such claims can be translated into real, useful benefits to those who would consider making changes in their gardening approaches, all the more so as these closely mimic Nature's ways.

It must be noted that Nature's ecosystems include both annuals and perennials (shoots, edible roots, fruits and flowers that continuously produce year after year). Aside from shrubs and fruit-bearing trees, there are more than a hundred perennial vegetable species that grows comfortably in North America.

Growing perennials brings so much to the table; you have the ability to create a very diverse garden that needs less attending and more time for harvests instead. And however you look at it, this is a great advantage compared to other grown farm items. You could even think of it as "zero-work gardening" if you wish. There are instances in some places where 11-year old perennial vegetable beds (with the help of added compost and mulch on a yearly basis) are still miraculously bearing food.

Growing perennial vegetables also extends every harvest season even without the aid of a greenhouse, cold frames, or other devices. You could readily harvest Jerusalem artichokes in the winter so long as you introduce enough mulch to keep the farm ground from freezing up.

In some regions, some perennial crop types (such as sorrel) are available as early as March, even as the snow is still melting away. And as perennials make up the bulk of the spring food harvest, the annual vegetables will come in next (after the springtime food harvest is finished of course).

Growing perennials doesn't mean you'll be giving up on some of our favorites, like peppers or tomatoes. You'll get useful and amazing benefits if you focus on perennial edibles. Just rethink your existing garden and introduce new and unused areas to become part of that garden.

Easy Maintenance

As already mentioned, growing perennials is low maintenance. Imagine growing vegetables that do not require much more than the same care we give to perennial shrubs and flowers. This means no annual planting and tilling as well. Perennials thrive just about anywhere. Once settled in the appropriate site and ideal climate, you can leave them alone. You can even choose to neglect them, as they are literately indestructible.

Established perennial vegetables are more resistant to diseases, weeds, pests, and drought most of the time. Amazingly, some perennials can take care of themselves so well that you might have to harvest them frequently, so they don't end up becoming weeds themselves. The best reason for growing perennial vegetables is the ease in cultivation and the high yield that follows.

The Practice Extends The Harvests

Growing perennial vegetables means more opportunities than growing annuals since you can grow many perennial items each season. This also means you'll have more food available to you throughout the year. You're never a slave to the seasons. You can plant small annual seedlings down into the vegetable garden and wait it out until the fury of the mid-summer heat is gone, perennial vegetables just go about their business. They are built for whatever season comes along.

Water Saving

The perennial plants will start adjusting to the climate in your garden, and they will not have a problem with finding their way to underground water. They will be able to develop strong and long roots that will go deep down and access the underground water. This will allow you to water them only a little and save on a lot of water.

This will also mean that missing a few weeks of watering owing to being on vacation will not mean the death of your perennials and only mean that they will still be waiting for you!

The Ability To Engage In Multiple Garden Functions

Perennial vegetable varieties are simply astounding. A good bunch of them are considered beautiful ornamental plants; they enhance every landscape. Some function as ground covers, hedges, or even erosion control intended for slopes. They can also climb trellises, providing shade for surrounding crops. Others even provide fertilization to their own surroundings including neighboring plants. They achieve this by introducing nitrogen into the soil.

There are even perennial vegetable varieties that provide habitats for beneficial insects/pollinators.

And it doesn't end there. There are great ecosystem benefits, too, especially when it comes to trees, as they slow down (to a certain degree) global warming effects by ensnaring atmospheric carbon dioxide. Perennial trees are also considered moderate micro-climates, encouraging moister and cooler conditions. A large concentration of perennial trees could help moderate regional climates in the same way.

The roots of perennials are designed to store nutrients and water that would, in other cases, be simply washed away. Perennials also provide animal and fungal life forms with a critical habitat. Many of these life forms offer significant benefits to gardens.

Variety

One of the biggest advantages of having perennials in your garden is that you will have a lot of variety available to you throughout the year. Just as one plant will finish producing a fruit, there will be another one that will be ready with its fruit. This will allow you to remain busy during every month of the year and a garden full of fruits that will only keep you happy for a long time.

Nutrition

When it comes to the perennials, they remain for so long inside the soil, that they develop a very complex root system. This system helps them access nutrition from even the darkest and deepest areas inside the soil and allows them to grow stronger and stronger. This will mean healthier plants capable of lasting several decades and you will not have to worry about replacing any of them. You will also not have to worry too much about having to add in any extra nutrients in the future, and the plants will only need water and sun to survive.

Building up the soil

Another great ecological benefit that we get from growing perennial vegetables is its positive effect on the soil. With these great soil builders, you don't need to till the ground anymore, as perennial vegetables help foster an intact and healthy soil food web.

As we all know, bare soil dries out fast, and wind and rain can easily find their marks through the erosion that would eventually follow, especially in sloped gardens. Tilling also kills off much of the soil food web's numerous beneficial elements, specifically the best mycorrhizae types (these beneficial fungi share the nutrients with surrounding crops). Well-mulched perennial vegetables need no more tilling, so long as they are already established on the ground.

The soil benefits of the perennial concept, however, are never limited to the absence of tillage. Perennial vegetables improve surrounding soil structure, soil porosity, organic matter, and the general ground's ability to hold water through the slow and steady rate of roots and leaves going through decomposition.

As perennials mature, they also aid in building topsoil and in sequestering atmospheric carbon.

What makes perennial vegetable gardens really stand out from other regular gardens is how they build up the soil just like Nature did. This is achieved by letting plants add significant organic matter without having to resort to tillage, and at the same time allowing worms a free hand in mixing the components together.

So what else can these remarkable plants do?

When Grown as Annuals

People also treat some perennials as annuals since they are logically much easier to care this way. A good example would be potatoes. Technically, the potato is a perennial, but we considered growing it as an annual since pressure from disease and pests in North America calls for rotating potatoes on a regular basis. But you can treat them as perennials and simply take good care of them. Potato plants can be quite moody, no doubt, but you must not give up on them and persist in maintaining the current crop and only rotate them if the soil is starting to turn bad.

Chapter 13: Preparing The Terrace

First and foremost, I thank you for downloading this book, and hope it rightfully serves the purpose of educating you on the topic of "Terrace Gardening".

When we think of growing crops our minds wander away to vast expanses of land and tractors tilling soil. We often wonder how farmers end up with hordes or produce just by sowing a few seeds in the ground. We then quickly realize that there will be more to do to grow crops than one can shake a stick at!

However, what if I told you, that you can grow these crops in the very confines of your terrace? Wouldn't that be a great revelation?

And, if you are itching to know more on how this can be made possible, then let me help you by diving straight into the basics of terrace gardening!

Terrace gardening refers to using your terrace as an area to grow flowers, vegetables, fruits etc. Your terrace can double up as a floral garden and all you need is a little space where the rays of the sun fall directly. It does not matter if you have a small terrace or a big one, as long as there is enough space to place a few pots or containers.

Let us now look at the various things that you will have to do, to prepare your humble terrace for gardening purposes.

Area

The very first thing that you must do is look for the best areas on your terrace, where you can carry out your gardening. The golden rule is to make use of the land that receives the maximum sunlight. If your terrace has scattered sunlight then you can decide and place your pots, or containers, by spreading them all around the terrace.

Wooden garden beds

Wooden garden beds are large wooden crates that you can lay out on your terrace and fill with soil. These will make for great plant beds, as they will allow you to have a large plot of soil dedicated to growing plants of your choice, and will also look like a real garden.

Containers

Containers can be placed on the terrace and make for a better choice owing to their small size and light weight. You will be able to move them around the garden as and when required. More on containers is explained in the next chapter.

Landscaping

Landscaping refers to planning the garden in such a way that it looks beautiful. For this, you need to bear in mind the basic aesthetics that will act as guiding principles for your terrace garden. When it comes to landscaping, you need to consider two main aspects; masses and voids. The masses will be your containers, tall plants, fountains, bird baths, tables, chairs etc. and your voids will be open spaces which you can either leave empty or grow low growing plants. You need to plan your garden structure in such a way that it incorporates both of these efficiently. You can try and have more of structural elements and only a few voids, and place them at strategic points.

You can choose to have fences separating each container or place them on stone, or metal, steps to add structure to your garden. You can choose to hang a few plants with the use of hangers and grow interesting ones such as the "spider plant", which will grow its leaves downwards.

You can size up your terrace and decide on the landscaping by making a mental image, or can take pictures of your garden and use an app that will allow you to place images over it. Once you make your choice, you can go ahead with the purchasing.

Remember, how you plan your terrace garden is entirely up to you, and you can choose a landscape depending on your taste. You can look for inspiration from books and websites but the final design call will be yours.

Chapter 14: What Is Verticial Gardening?

With the growing population and increased industrialization taking place in the world today, there is less and less garden space available. Vertical gardening is a type of innovative gardening that uses non-traditional growing spaces.

Vertical gardening is a highly productive technique that gives gardeners the option of choosing many simple and effective methods. Since most plants tend to grow outward, this type of gardening is about training plants to grow upward so that you can save space.

Vertical gardening is about growing up or down. It also involves stacking techniques, color designs and a variety of shapes and textures. It is 3D gardening that takes advantage of vertical plans to grow an assortment of plants in both big and small spaces. When you train your plants to grow vertically, you not only save space but you also make it easier to harvest them. What's more, you provide an ideal condition for growing because the circulation of air is better when plants are off the ground. You also keep them away from mold, crawling pests, insects, and other soil-borne plant ailments.

It can be a very interesting venture: from creating a simple structure to an elaborate garden piece. You can use common hanging baskets, pots or shelves. You can make frame structures and cross shelves. Wooden trellises, metal trellises, plastic containers, wooden frames or any combination of materials will make you vertical garden look great.

A plus side to vertical gardening is that you can maximize the potential available space for gardening. It is the perfect solution if you have limited space. If you live in an urban area, a vertical garden can help reduce air pollution. You can also use your vertical garden to create some privacy. A vertical garden will be most useful for people that have health and mobility problems because these gardens are easily accessible for caring and harvesting.

In the following chapters, you will find more detailed information on the benefits of vertical gardening in today's world. You will also learn about different kinds of vertical gardening set-ups and how to make them work for you.

Chapter 15: Landscaping – An Overview

Before you get started with landscaping, there are few things that need to be taken into consideration. In this chapter, we have touched on the preliminary things that need to be taken care of before you venture into finishing your garden planning.

Your abilities

Before you begin with the landscaping, understand where your strengths lie. Take stock of your abilities when it comes to gardening. If you have had any prior experience when it comes to gardening or construction, make a list of your strengths, as these will help you to decide what is doable. You might wonder why this is of any relevance. When you take stock of your abilities when it comes to gardening as well as landscaping, it makes it easier to decide if you need to enlist the help of a professional or not. It also determines the time and effort that you need to invest in the entire process. Apart from your gardening skills, you have to take into consideration your sense of color and texture. Since landscaping is all about the magic of colors and textures placed side by side, it is important that you have a clear sense of how you want your garden to look before you start working on it.

Commitment

Landscaping your garden can be a time-consuming process. It might look simple and exciting in the beginning, but it requires a good amount of effort on your part, especially if you have decided to do it all by yourself. Do not commit to landscaping if you can't cope with the hard labor involved. Rest assured that your hard labor will be rewarded but be aware also that it's going to require physical input. Understand what this task demands of you before you start, as you may need help with the physical aspects and hard landscaping.

Planning

Nothing is as important as a sound plan when it comes to landscaping. Why is this so relevant? When it comes to landscaping, if you don't have a clear idea of how you want your garden to look, your efforts will be futile. When we refer to planning, it means two things – planning the way you want your garden to look and planning your time to achieve the work required to get it into shape.

As mentioned earlier, landscaping is a time-consuming process. Unless you plan and allocate your time for it properly, you would not be able to complete the process within the stipulated time. Time is of the essence, especially when you are seeking professional help. You cannot afford to waste time, for it would cost you more than you think. Even if you are not seeking professional help, you cannot go about it without allocating proper time for it.

When you don't allow a specific amount of time for this, the entire process of landscaping will drag on for months. You do not want your garden to look unfinished and messy for months, do you? Another area of concern is you would have to spend a lot of time removing the weeds and cleaning up your garden for landscaping it. As some of the plants are seasonal, should you wish to incorporate them in your garden, you should plan for their availability during the time you are designing your garden.

Apart from the time, you need to plan the layout of your garden. Landscaping is not based on the trial and error method. It is important that you have a clear idea upfront as to how to go about designing your garden. This will help you analyze the time and cost required to achieve the desired result. Decide the space requirements for your garden at the planning stage. If there are space constraints, you will be able to decide the kind of garden that you wish to have. If you need to invest in hard landscaping, you will need to estimate the cost for this, so it's essential that you have measurements and a good idea of the materials that you need.

Colors and textures

As mentioned earlier, colors and textures play an important role in making the landscaping look effective, and your garden look vibrant. Pick out the color scheme carefully. Landscaping is not about growing plants in all possible colors. It's about making a garden look elegant even if there aren't many colors. Bear in mind that not all plants will look the same in all seasons. Choose your plants in such a fashion that they adhere to a certain color scheme during a specific season as it is not possible to make your garden look colorful during all seasons. It is worthwhile listing the flowers and noting down the seasons when you can expect flowers to appear.

Textures add an interesting twist to the way your garden looks. Arrange your plants in such a fashion that there is some continuity when it comes to the textural aspect. For instance, it would look spectacular if you plant your rose bushes in the same row. This will look esthetically beautiful and also help you in tending to them in an effective fashion.

Ambiance

Apart from the esthetic features of your garden, the ambiance also has to be taken into consideration. The question that you should ask yourself is "What should I feel when I step into my garden?" For instance, if you wish to have a peaceful and soothing ambiance, you could make room for a small fountain in your garden or a place to sit and enjoy it.

Other things that you could add to your garden to influence the ambiance of it may range from interesting sculptures to walkways, lightings, etc. If you are going to invest in lighting, ensure that you have a clear idea of what you want the lights to illuminate. For example, you may be thinking of pathways or even of highlighting certain species of plants. Choose them wisely and make sure that if underground wiring is required, this is planned for in advance. Many people use solar power these days, which doesn't require underground wiring.

Understanding your plants

An important aspect of your garden is the kind of plants that you wish to grow.

Landscaping is not about growing all kinds of plants together. It's all about choosing those plants that are compatible in term of needs, as well as that complement each other esthetically. Why is it important that you understand your plants? Sooner or later, you will realize that tending to these plants requires a lot of time and effort. If you choose companion plants, half your burden is reduced.

Understand what the requirements are when it comes to the different kinds of plants. Some might need a lot of sunshine while others might grow well even in the shade. Landscaping is all about placing your plants in a strategic way that, apart from making your garden look beautiful, makes it easier for you to maintain it.

Do as much research as you can. List of all the requirements associated with the various plants. Choose those plants that are possible for you to tend easily rather than giving yourself hard work. A lot of time has to be invested in tending to certain species. As mentioned earlier, the time factor has to be taken into consideration.

Be open to changes

You might have to change the way your garden looks from time to time. Understand that your landscaping is not a permanent process. You might have to change some elements of your garden to suit the various seasons or to give your garden a new look. Be prepared for the changes and expect your garden to evolve.

There can be multiple reasons that might be the cause for the changes that you may have to make to the existing landscape. Sometimes, the plants you choose might be high maintenance, and you might want to replace them with different varieties. Sometimes, certain kinds of plants become infected by bacterial diseases, despite your best efforts. Hence, you could hire a professional who would be able to advise you beforehand about the probable scenarios that might require you to invest time and effort to make the requisite changes to your landscape. This will help you to take precautionary steps as well as being prepared to make the changes, if and when required.

Get your family on board

It is important that you get your family on board with the whole idea of landscaping your garden. As mentioned earlier, landscaping is a time-consuming process and requires a lot of manual labor. Unless you get the support of your family, it will most certainly be a Herculean task.

Keeping the initial landscaping aside, you would need an extra pair of hands in maintaining the beauty of your garden. Some families even allot different chores within the garden to family members, and this is worth thinking about.

These are the preliminary things that have to be taken into consideration before you take up a time-consuming yet rewarding process like landscaping!

Chapter 16: Understanding Homesteading

In this fast-paced technology driven world, the idea of living life at a slow and relaxing pace has started to gain popularity and acceptance. Rising inflation, overdependence on technology, shortage of resources, pesticides ridden fruits and vegetables, and not-a-moment-to-catch-my-breath lifestyle have pushed a number of people into looking at homesteading as a viable lifestyle. Although homesteading is certainly not a new concept, the ideas and concepts of urban homesteading has started to gain traction with both the young and the urban population.

Homesteading way of life was very common in the past and people have been consistently growing fruits and vegetables in their backyard from times immemorial.

Moreover, the concept of raising chicken in the backyard pen is not uncommon either. While the idea of homesteading and self-sufficiency might not be new, the ways in which homesteading is practiced has certainly undergone a drastic change. In the past, homesteaders spent years undertaking backbreaking tasks of plowing, tilling and harvesting farms carved out of complete wilderness. They stayed away from modern day amenities and tools. Although, present day homesteaders too undertake physically exhaustive tasks, they are, nevertheless, not as grueling as the olden-day tasks. But, let this not fool you as homesteading – present or past – is taxing if you do not have the right aptitude to live your life without a number of so-called 'basic' amenities that we take for granted.

A large number of people are attracted towards homesteading because it helps keep unhealthy and harmful chemicals out of the food chain. Turning to gardening is the only way to ensure that each and every one of us has access to wholesome and less-contaminated food. Moreover, people have gone further and have ensured that chemicals do not find their way into their personal lives as well. With every action they take, homesteaders make sure that they do not harm themselves, their co-beings, the Earth and the future generations. Call it what you may – green movement, eco conscious or going green – the basic idea that defines homesteading is self-sufficiency and environmental responsibility. Homesteading, as difficult and backbreaking it might seem initially, is the first step towards a happier, healthier and satisfying lifestyle.

Urban homesteading is not a new concept or an idea; in fact, homesteading is as old as the mountains. Before people started buying bread and eggs from stores, everyone raised poultry in their backyards and baked bread at their homes. Homesteading is an ancient concept; however, urban homesteading has revived the old techniques of self-sufficiency and adapted them to suit the urban dwellers' needs. Urban homesteading is not a single concept; it is a collection of various techniques and practices. It includes growing vegetables and fruits, raising animals, preserving food, making bread, cheese and yogurt at home, spinning and knitting, making cleaning products, using solar and wind energy, conserving water and making fertilizers and compost. The one concept that holds urban and rural homesteading is the idea of providing for self, resisting the temptation to binge consumption, consuming products made at home, creating products rather than purchasing mass-produced products from stores.

Here are the facts this book contains:

Grow your own fruits and vegetables.

Raise farm animals for food

Use alternative sources of energy – renewable energy

Rethink transportation by using bicycles or walking to work

Make efforts to reduce waste and also repurpose waste

Rainwater harvesting

Do your housework yourself

Learn to knit, mend, do repairs and learn using basic tools and techniques

Make food at home such as cheese, bread and yogurt

Live in a simple and self-sufficient manner.

Why Homesteading is a good decision

Broadly defined, Home steading is a lifestyle of self-sufficiency and it is characterized by subsistence agriculture and it's a household compound for a single extended family.

Some of the benefits that we get when we choose homesteading are:

Quality of food and life: Regardless of the reasons homesteaders provide for living a life of self-sufficiency, at the end of the day, quality of food and quality of life is the main reasons why they chose this way of life. Homemade yogurt and eggs have a taste that leaves your mouth salivating for more. Homemade bread is so soft and fresh that the store-bought fresh seems tasteless in comparison. Good quality food helps us for a better life style.

Happy and Healthy Life: There is a number of health benefits associated with homesteading. The food you produce, undoubtedly, has a number of health benefits than mass-produced foods. Eggs, bread, meat and other homemade foods have their nutrients intact while mass-produced food items tend to lose out on essential nutrients as they sit in the box waiting for you in the supermarket. Moreover, your backyard chicks and goats tend to feast on a variety of healthy foods that helps them produce nutrient-rich food.

In addition to being nutrient rich, home grown fruits and vegetables do not have harmful pesticides and chemicals in them. Since home grown food are not genetically modified or artificially ripened, they retain their natural color, taste and nutrients. A number of diseases that result from factory farming such as E.coli, salmonella and other viruses are eliminated in homegrown foods.

The health benefits of homesteading are not limited to food; in fact, the amount of exercise you get also helps you lead a healthy life. The amount of work involved in homesteading is exceptionally beneficially to your body. Even if you are into urban homesteading, you get a lot of physical exercise which is great for your health and general well-being.

Economically Beneficial: Baking your own bread is way cheaper than buying a loaf of bread from the nearby supermarket. Some people might tell you that homesteading involves investing in a lot of fancy gadgets and tools; however, this is completely not true. Making your own soap, bread, eggs, meat and bread goes a long way in helping you save a lot of money. In fact, homesteading also involves various ways of preserving food items in an environmentally friendly manner.

You can easily grow a container garden using spare containers at home or also look for square foot gardening techniques.

Environmental Friendly: Our technology-enriched lifestyle has been consistently taxing our planet's resources so much that we are on the verge of exhausting a number of non-renewable resources. Most of us assume that if we shift from travelling in cars to travelling in public transport or going in for carpooling, you are saving the planet. It is true that carpooling and travelling in public transportation helps save gallons of oil, we should also understand that it is not enough to help save the planet. Transporting fruits, vegetables and other food products from the farm to our home consumes hundreds of gallons of oil. Homesteading and gardening can help save the planet in a number of other ways too. Factory farming and mass-manufacturing of products is consuming a lot of resources. In fact, the toxins from these farms and factories are choking our natural water and soil resources. They are harming the earth's repair and restoration efforts. However, this does not mean that you have to throw up your hands in utter exasperation and give up hope for a better future. You don't even have to run off into a cave or give up your fancy home in the city. Urban homesteading helps you retain your home in the city and continue to enrich your life and save the environment as well.

Creating a Sense of Togetherness: The idea of self-sufficiency and togetherness seem poles apart and contradictory. However, there are more related to each other than we assume. When you take up urban homesteading, you are indirectly encouraging others in your community to join hands in making the world a much better place to live. You will be surprised to learn that a number of people would be more than willing to help you in your endeavors. Self-sufficiency is not about providing only for self or isolating from others. In fact, urban homesteading is being taken up as a community effort in a number of places.

Personally Gratifying: There is nothing more gratifying that seeing a beautiful bunch of carrots or baking a large loaf of bread – all by you. The sense of satisfaction and pride you get by growing your own food, raising goats and chickens and making your own soaps and other utilities cannot be compared with buying them from the supermarket. You achieve a deep sense of satisfaction, achievement, and also develop a positive and healthy attitude towards life.

Urban Homesteading Vs Rural Homesteading

Both urban and rural homesteading offers a great sense of satisfaction of doing things by ourselves. Growing fruits and vegetables in a backyard garden, cooking them, building furniture and tools for our homes, and also learning new techniques of self-sufficiency and re-learning old and forgotten skills is homesteading these days. Homesteading provides a lot of independence and choices. It protects us from debt crisis, offers more choices for pursuing hobbies and interests, offers greater security in the times of economic slowdown and recession, and protects us from environmental hazards.

While homesteading throws up a picture of living in the countryside with vast (read acres) areas of land waiting to be tilled and plowed, it is nothing more than just a daytime fantasy. In fact, rural homesteading is possible only for people who have the luxury of land and time. If you are living in the city, homesteading might seem like a distant impossible dream. Giving up on amenities like cell phone, internet, home delivery, garbage pickup, electricity, gas, near-by neighbors and easy transportation might seem like a heavy toll to pay. Living in the countryside might be peaceful, calm and more laid-back; however, this is not for everyone.

Most manuals on homesteading will tell you that you have to give up the luxuries of the city, pack your bags and settle down on a farm to take up homesteading. In fact, many homesteading experts also talk about gardening and raising farm animals on acres of land. The abundance and availability of land will soon become a burden when you don't know what to do with it. Just because you don't have an acre of land to call your own, don't give up on homesteading. You can continue to stay self-sufficient with urban homesteading. Even with a single square foot of land in the city or a balcony to call your own, you can grow your favorite fruits and vegetables and live a healthy life. If you have the luxury of land somewhere in the countryside, and are willing to give up the pleasures of the city, you are welcome to try rural homesteading. However, if space is a constraint and you don't want to lose your city life, you can try urban homesteading and enjoy the same benefits of rural living.

Homesteading and Permaculture

Homesteading and permaculture are related to one another; they propagate the concepts of self-sufficiency, care for the planet, people and returning natural resources to the planet. It is the concept of sustainable method of agriculture. Permaculture philosophy is working with nature and not working against its principles. It is the idea of looking at the landscape of a place, understand the functions of species and bring various pieces together to create one better product. Permaculture helps reduce waste, minimize labor and input of energy into making products. It is about bringing all the pieces of a concept together so that maximum benefits are availed from it.

Permaculture is an extended branch of ecological and environmental design.

Homesteading - A social, economic and lifestyle choice

To completely understand the concepts of homesteading, you should first understand its roots and reasons for its popularity. Back in 1862, the U.S. government offered nearly 160 acres of free land to people who promised to live on it successfully for years. Many families staked their claim to this land and started growing crops, raising animals, cultivating land, and took care of the household using homemade things.

The Homestead Act of 1862 was seen as an effort by the government of U.S. to populate previously undesired parts of land. Nations that were engaged in nation building, started enticing people to populate and cultivate on these pieces of land and develop self-sustenance methods. More Homestead acts were initiated in the late 19th and early 20th centuries to drive nation building and populating specific areas of the nation. A renewed interest in homesteading started to be seen in the 1930's and 1940's.

Homesteading, in addition to being a social process of creating self-sufficiency, is an economic choice to ensure independence and self-reliance. Homesteading not only allows you to produce food on your own, it also helps you sell your produce – food and other products – to others to help improve your financial status.

Homesteading is a lifestyle choice for many, and a number of people who are homesteading have expressed a deep sense of satisfaction and contentment with their lifestyle and standard of living. They feel that their way of life is far more healthy, satisfying and rewarding than the normal urban ways of life. Urban

Homesteading is not a watered-down version of rural homesteading; in fact, it is a full-fledged concept that has a number of benefits.

Chapter 17: Helpful Tips In Gardening

It is not easy but you can definitely produce your own food no matter where you live. Sprouts in mason jars in the kitchen, herbs in pots by the window, small garden beds in your backyard, to a sprawling country vegetable and flower garden; everyone can grow something. All you need to do now is decide what works for you based on where you are, what you want, and what you have.

Tips for Aspiring Gardeners

Grow what you would eat. If you won't eat it, then don't plant it. Plant only the fruits or vegetables that you and your family like.

Spend time in your garden. Be prepared to spend anywhere from a few minutes to a several hours in your garden daily. If you are not fully prepared to commit time to your plants, it might be better to stick to low maintenance herbs or sprouts or buy stuff from the farmers' market, which is perfectly okay, but kind of defeats the purpose of self-reliance.

Start small. Expand as you go along. A small well-taken-care-of garden is better than a large chunk of land full of weird looking poorly tended plants.

Test your soil. You do not want a bunch of dead plants. Testing will help you determine the pH level of the soil for optimum results.

Find your seed source. Seeds bloom into the food you will eat. Check out a company before ordering seeds or try out different companies before settling on one.

Grow your garden up not out. You can grow more crops in less space. Grow your crops vertically using trellis or fences.

Use organic pest control. Healthy plants are less likely to be targeted by bugs.

Invest in high-quality tools and learn how to use and take care of them.

Take advantage of weeds. Do not just remove and discard them. Some of these weeds may be medicinal or edible. You will never know unless you teach you weeds.

Enjoy the fun part. Start planting; stick the seeds in the soil. Do not forget to water your plants.

Compost and Fertilizers

Most gardeners recommended that you make your own compost. Compost is natural fertilizer for the soil, so it's also best that you make use of ingredients that are just around you. This way, you'd know that your plants won't be bombarded with pesticides.

Basically, you can start with using brown and green materials, but make sure to use more green than brown. Other ingredients you could include are newspaper bits, old flower heads, tea bags, peelings, and pruning.

Make sure that you use the largest compost bin you have, so compost wouldn't be too smelly. If you don't have anything large, go for a compact worm bin. Remember that it's also best to add compost each time you plant, and each time you harvest, as well.

Now, if you're going to use Fertilizers, make sure that you only use organic ones. Only use fertilizer when plants show they need some sprucing up, such as when they begin to set fruit, when buds appear, or even when you're about to plant them and the weather's not really nice.

Examples of Organic Fertilizers include Canola Meal, which is easy to spread and extremely lightweight. Make sure that you properly till it into the soil, though, so that it wouldn't get to attract mice and other insects.

Companion Planting Is Okay

When it comes to Companion Planting, what you have to keep in mind is that you need to keep crops near scented plants, so that insects and weeds would not be around them. When you have scented plants around, insects get to be distracted, which would also keep the plants safe from diseases and let them grow properly.

Speaking of insects, you could kill them by using parasitic wasps, or biological controls, that you can mostly get from online gardening stores. Here are sample suggestions for companion planting:

Cucumbers should be planted near corn, and beans. Keep them away from tomatoes.

Sweet Corn grows well with cucumbers, dill, cabbage, onions, and lettuce.

Eggplants are best planted with marigold, thyme, tarragon, spinach, peas, pole beans, bush beans, and amaranth.

Melons are best planted near corn, squash, radish, and pumpkin.

Peppers should be planted near tomatoes, rosemary, parsley, oregano, and basil.

Cilantro naturally repels insects away, so you could place them near most plants, especially radish, spinach, potatoes, and anise. Keep them away from Fennel as fennel dries cilantro out.

Basil grows well when planted with tomatoes.

Kale is best planted with cabbage, nasturtiums, onions, marigolds, cucumbers, and celery.

Lettuce and Dill go perfectly together!

Swiss Chard is best planted next to peppers.

Sage is best for repelling beetles and cabbage moths. They're best planted next to carrots, rosemary, cauliflower, and broccoli.

Tomatoes are best planted next to celery, carrots, beans, basil, and asparagus.

Radish is best planted next to cucumbers and corn.

Strawberries grow well when planted next to thyme, spinach, onions, lettuce, and beans.

Watermelon also grows well with corn, as well as with sunflowers and peas.

Crop Rotation Is Important

This also has a lot to do with companion planting, and arranging plants in a way that all of them would get enough sunlight and grow well.

What you have to keep in mind is that it's best to let heavy feeders stay near heavy givers, followed by light feeders, and vice versa.

Watering Plants

Watering Plants at the right times also make it easy for you to help your plants grow properly. It should be done either early in the morning, or late in the afternoon. Remember that plants need at least an inch of water per week, or around an hour of sprinkling.

Control Weeds

Weeds are a definite no-no.

Make sure that you destroy weeds by spreading some bark mulch, composted straw, or leaf mulch across the soil. Then, when you see weeds appear, immediately pull them out or use a hoe to prevent them from seeding.

Weeding should be done in the late afternoon to early evening. Doing so when the sun is high in the sky would just make water evaporate, and in turn, might damage your plants. Weeding is also essential because it prevents nutrient competition from happening.

Make sure to discard tough weeds and to compose weed seedlings so that they won't propagate anymore. Weeding after watering could also be good.

Harvest Properly

Now, when you're about to harvest, make sure you do it at the right time, too. This means that you have to do it in the morning, especially when dealing with cucumbers, spinach, and lettuce. As for root crops, you have to do it late in the afternoon so moisture would be intact.

Inspect Plants Regularly

It's best to check your plants regularly, just to see how they are, instead of waiting for something terrible to happen before spending time in the garden again. By doing so, you get to prevent infestation from happening, and you also get to make sure that they'll be able to grow the best way they can!

Chapter 18: Harvesting And Maintenance

The most exciting and fulfilling part of backyard gardening is the harvest. This refers to when the vegetables are ripe and ready to make the effortless journey from the ground to the oven or cupboard.

Harvesting

Knowing how and when to harvest your fruit and vegetables is just as essential as knowing how to sew them. Each vegetable plant has a time frame for ideal harvesting. While some vegetables are tough enough to endure a long harvest, others can turn bitter and spoilt overnight.

There's a huge amount of common sense that the gardener needs to apply when deciding on harvesting dates. It's not as simple as checking your calendar. Good growth depends on many factors such as temperature and soil quality, and so the timings can vary from year to year. The best way to decide when a vegetable is ready for harvest is by observing its characteristics. It can take practise to get this right, so be patient and keep a journal of any basic observations that need noting for next time.

It's crucial to keep track of what is in the ground, and keep an eye on seed packet instructions. Most vegetables are at the height of tenderness and taste when they are still quite small. Courgettes, for example, are best when they are no more than seven inches long otherwise they can taste woody and rubbery. Lettuce leaves can also be picked as early as desired.

When harvesting the crops, it's important to look out for signs of trouble. Yellow or browning leaves or rotting flesh can cause further issues for the other crops so remove any problems that are encountered.

Root vegetables (carrots, potatoes, radishes etc), can be checked for readiness by loosening the soil and gently pulling up the vegetable to check its size. Again, root vegetables are best eaten young, otherwise their taste and texture can become a tad unappealing. You might be interested to know that root vegetables can be stored in the ground as soon as the tops die, as long as the ground is oversee by a thick layer or leaves, straw or mulch. This is a good tip for those short on storage.

The best time to harvest vegetables is in the morning. This is when they have the most water retention. Most importantly, don't forget your basket and pruners!

Storage

Before harvesting, consider storage. You cannot cook everything at once. One option is to freeze the vegetables or store them in a cellar. It's best to harvest as close to the time you're going to eat or preserve the vegetables as possible to retain flavour and nutrients.

For a longer root vegetable storage life, dig up the vegetables after a few straight days of dry weather, and allow the produce to sit in the sun for a few hours after being pulled from the ground. This will kill the root hairs, making the plant redundant, and the soil on the roots will fall off with ease. Never wash root vegetables before storing them. For the best quality taste, wash the vegetables just before using them.

It goes without saying that you should only store the best vegetables. Ones that are damaged by insects or showing signs of rotting they can spread disease to other vegetables and this will destroy the entire bunch. Bruised vegetables should be eaten as a priority as this too can lead to rot.

Conditions for healthy storage should be a cool temperatures to help prevent moisture loss. Bacteria that's growing on the vegetables will not grow or reproduce as quickly if the temperature is low. It may also be worth investing in a humidity gauge, something that can measure the levels of humidity in the room. 80 per cent humidity is ideal. If you own polyethylene bags, these can hold vegetables safely, in order to retain moisture. Finally, the vegetables need to breathe while in storage, so air circulation and ventilation is recommended.

Maintenance

Following the first harvest, it's possible to re-plant straight away and so the cycle can continue. During dry season, remember the garden will require extra watering.

If you plan to plant something new every week or two, a continuous harvest will manifest for all-year-round produce. It takes some skill to pick the right crops, and there will be a lot of learning and practise involved.

Pests and disease are an all-year-round problem for backyard gardeners. Fences should be built to deter rabbits (make sure holes in your garden fence are filled). Ideally the fence should reach 6 inches under the soil, as rabbits are skilled diggers.

Netting and row covers, or light transparent plastic can prevent bugs and insects from feasting on growing plants.

To reduce the risk of fungus, try to only water the soil instead of the leaves of the plant. Sprinklers are not precise enough and sometimes increase the risk of fungal disease, so if this is a problem, switching to a watering can may be the solution. If a plant looks diseased, remove it immediately and throw it away (do not compost it). Tools may need to be disinfected if they've been used on diseased plants.

Weeds are trouble. They rob the vegetables of their space, ability to breathe and light. Every few days, check the garden for weeds. Using your hand trowel to remove them when you see them.

Take out your dead. This might sound rather sinister, but it's so important that dead stems, leaves, vegetables and matter are disposed of or composted.

Crop Rotation

It's advisable to move the plants around the garden every year or two. This can drastically minimise the likelihood of disease, as well as pests and animals gaining a permanent home in the garden.

Once you have harvested your crop, put the spent plant and other vegetable matter into your compost pile so that it can be recycled into your garden again, next spring.

Crop rotation within the vegetable garden means planting the same crop in the same place only once every three years. This policy ensures that the same garden vegetables will not deplete the same nutrients year after year. It can also help foil any insect pests or disease pathogens that might be lurking in the soil after the crop is harvested.

Finally, we end up where we started. The full circle of backyard gardening can remain continuous and productive as long as the effort of the gardener remains consistent also. Vegetable gardening is highly rewarding, and hopefully enjoyable. It can become an art form once the basic techniques are perfected, with new varieties of crops to choose from, some of which are more complicated to grow. An important way of maintaining the hard work is to join a community group or online forum to share and receive further tips and tricks for success. Why not host a dinner party using all of your home grown food or hand some beans and carrots out to neighbours to try in their stew? Gardening has, after all, the profound ability to connect people not only to their food but to their community too.

Chapter 19: Apprenticeships

If you are still hesitant about the idea, and you want to have a better look at the farming business, apprenticeships in farming seem to be highly valued and educational. The majority of young farmers made their first steps as apprentices.

It is not paid significantly, but you will learn a lot about the farm business. Farming is hard work, and that is not a secret so be aware that you will do a lot of quite demanding tasks. Farming as many other businesses has a hierarchy, so you have to work your way up. The bright side is that you work outside, and you have a lot of space for movement. It is hard work, but it is not tedious as working in an office.

Those who consider entering a farm have a lot of dilemma by not being sure what is the product they want to grow, plant or maybe they would breed animals. Are they fans of value-added goods and/or food-processing? The apprenticeship can help them figure out their preferences.

As an apprentice, you should observe carefully what the farmer workers do. One of the basic equipment you should bring is a sunhat, sunglasses, pocket knife, work gloves, flashlight, thermos, sleeping bag, medical kit, work boots, rain boots, wool sweater, tent, high-energy candy like chocolate bars. Apprentices will learn the most through the one-on-one approach, and they have to be monitored closely because of the valuable equipment they could damage due to inexperience.

As we mentioned already above, a great percentage of farmers do not own land, but rent it. Many beginner farmers are concerned with the land issue. They think that land ownership is the starting point.

In reality, it is not the case. Even some authors on small farming advise against the land purchase if you have to sink into debt. You can buy land at a later stage when you feel confident about your incomes that became steady.

Conclusion

Everybody enjoys hobbies throughout their leisure time. Some people might have more than one hobby. Well, here's one among us for those gardeners and arborists. Consider hydroponic gardening indoors as an entertaining hobby. You will enjoy indoor hydroponic gardening if you love gardens and make things grow.

Hydroponic gardening is the same as regular planting unless there is no mess at all. Indoor hydroponic gardening has no soil. Have you ever seen the famous Babylon Hanging Gardens? This is one of the world's Seven Wonders and is probably the earliest evidence of our indoor hydroponic gardening in human history.

Very few people now have the resources to produce something as luxuriant as this earthly wonder, but in a hydroponic greenhouse, we can grow our own minibar. It is the same as a regular greenhouse, but hydroponic because all plants are grown with water, light and air.

That is false. That is right. There is no need for soil. This is exactly what indoor hydroponic gardening is about. Growing in a hydroponic greenhouse, your favorite fruits and vegetables, is the latest fad among gardeners. Everything you need and if you really want to go to the local pond and garden shop and

www.ingramcontent.com/pod-product-compliance
Lightning Source LLC
Chambersburg PA
CBHW071844080526
44589CB00012B/1099